Super Explorers

EXPLORING TROPICAL RAINFORESTS

T0182565

Krista Kagume

Contents

What are Rainforests?

Rainforests are rich, wet woods full of tall trees and twisting vines. Unusual animals live among the lush, green plants. Giant bugs crawl on the mossy ground, and strange sounds are heard all around.

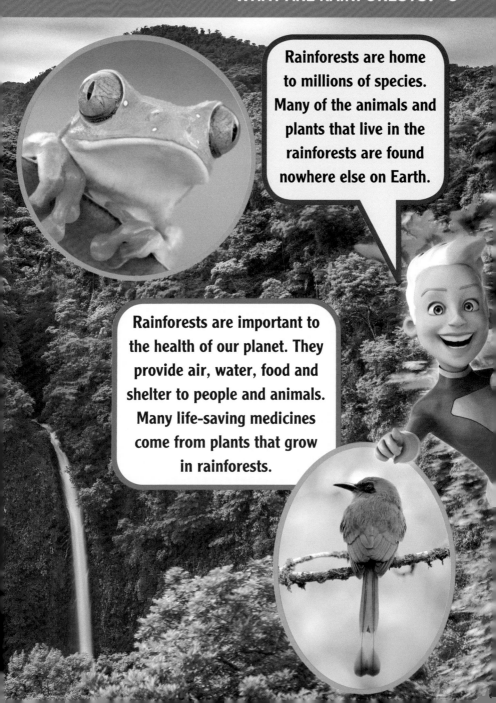

Rainforests are home to millions of species. Many of the animals and plants that live in the rainforests are found nowhere else on Earth.

Rainforests are important to the health of our planet. They provide air, water, food and shelter to people and animals. Many life-saving medicines come from plants that grow in rainforests.

Where are Rainforests?

Most rainforests grow in warm areas near the equator, like in Central and South America, Africa and Southeast Asia. These are called tropical rainforests. The animals and plants in this book live and grow in tropical rainforests.

CLIMATE ZONES

- Equatorial
- Tropical
- Temperate
- Polar
- Subequatorial
- Subtropical
- Subpolar

Arctic Circle 66°N

Tropic of Cancer 23°N

Equator 0°

Tropic of Capricorn 23°S

Antarctic Circle 66°S

The largest tropical rainforest in the world is the Amazon rainforest in South America. It's about two-thirds as big as the United States!

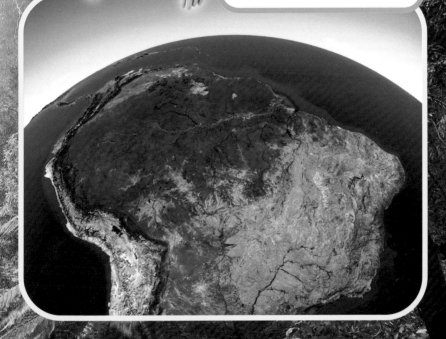

Some rainforests grow in cooler places, near the ocean. These are called temperate rainforests. The Pacific temperate rainforest is the largest on earth. It is found on the west coast of North America.

Rainy and Hot, Every Day!

It rains almost every day in the rainforest. There is a huge amount of rain!

Most rainforests get 6 feet (2 m) of rain each year. That's as much rain as the height of a door. Some get as much as 30 feet (9m) of rain each year. That's as tall as a 3-story building!

The temperature is always warm in the tropical rainforest, even at night. The air feels wet and steamy, like a bathroom after a hot shower. It feels like summer all year-round.

Everything Is Connected

A rainforest is a complex ecosystem. An ecosystem is a community of living and non-living things in a specific area.

An ecosystem can be any size. A puddle can be an ecosystem, and so can an ocean. Your house can be one, too!

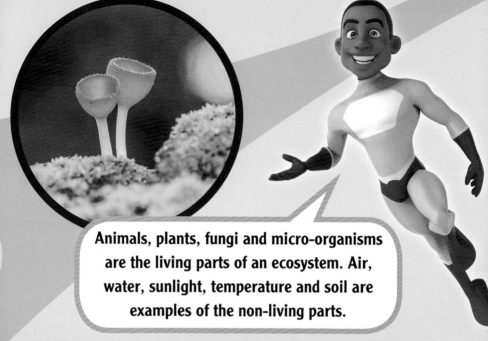

Animals, plants, fungi and micro-organisms are the living parts of an ecosystem. Air, water, sunlight, temperature and soil are examples of the non-living parts.

All parts of an ecosystem are connected. Living and non-living things work together to keep the rainforest in balance.

Bright Colors

Scarlet Macaws

Many colorful creatures live in the rainforest. Animals and plants use color in many ways. Bright colors are easy to see. Sometimes color helps an animal stand out or attract a mate.

Plants use color in surprising ways. There are many shades of green in the rainforest, but many plants have red flowers. Red attracts birds and insects that pollinate the flowers.

Reticulated Poison Dart Frog

Some animals use color to warn predators not to eat them. Poison dart frogs have poisonous skin. If an animal eats a dart frog, it will get sick.

Strawberry Poison Dart Frog

River Highways

The Amazon River is one of the longest rivers in the world. It is 4000 miles (6440 km) long. More than 1000 smaller streams feed into this massive river. Big ships from the ocean can sail far up the Amazon River.

One way to see the rainforest is by boat. People often use the rivers like highways to travel through the rainforest.

The tangled plants growing by the river are very thick, and people must cut their way through. This overgrown vegetation is called a jungle. The first explorers named the rainforests jungles.

Mangroves are trees that grow along the muddy riverbanks and coastal areas. They are the only trees in the world that can grow in saltwater.

Marvelous Mangroves

These trees have tall, tangled roots that can rise above the water. Mangrove trees look like they're standing on stilts!

Mangroves add oxygen to the air we breathe. Their roots also help keep the riverbank from washing away. The tangled, underwater roots are a perfect place for fish to hide. All kinds of creatures, from tiny fish and turtles to sharks, use the mangroves to raise their young.

Thousands of fish and animals live in rainforest rivers or on the riverbanks. If you take a boat ride up the Amazon River, you might see colorful birds and bizarre animals.

Teeming with Life

Capybaras live along the riverbanks. These big rodents look a bit like giant guinea pigs. They are related to squirrels and muskrats.

The **giant river otter** is the largest otter on earth. It lives in slow-moving rivers or creeks of South America and feeds on fish and crustaceans.

The otter's extra-sensitive whiskers can feel movements in the water, helping it to find prey.

Big and Powerful

Large rivers like the Amazon River are home to many animals. The anaconda is the largest, longest and heaviest snake in world. This powerful constrictor lives in rivers and preys on animals such as capybaras and tapirs. It coils around its victim, crushing it to death and then swallowing it whole.

After a meal, an anaconda may have a big bulge as it slowly digests its prey.

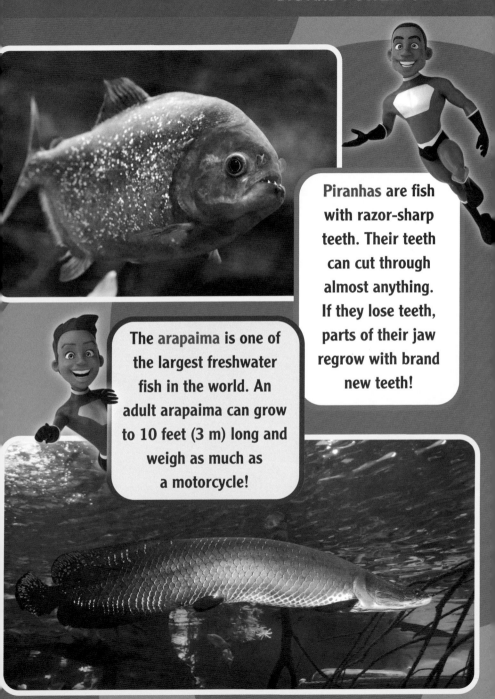

Piranhas are fish with razor-sharp teeth. Their teeth can cut through almost anything. If they lose teeth, parts of their jaw regrow with brand new teeth!

The arapaima is one of the largest freshwater fish in the world. An adult arapaima can grow to 10 feet (3 m) long and weigh as much as a motorcycle!

Smart and Friendly

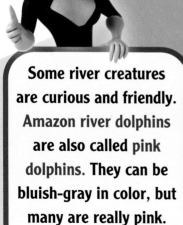

Some river creatures are curious and friendly. Amazon river dolphins are also called pink dolphins. They can be bluish-gray in color, but many are really pink. When they are excited, they get even pinker!

Dolphins usually live in ocean saltwater, but the pink dolphin lives in freshwater rivers. It uses its long, thin snout to poke around the river bottom for food.

Dolphins are not fish. They are mammals. These creatures can stay underwater for a long time, but they must come to the surface to breathe air. They breathe through a blowhole that is on top of their head!

Unusual River Birds

The jabiru stork is the tallest flying bird in South America. Large groups of storks can be found near water, feeding on fish and frogs.

These amazing birds build huge nests that are 10 feet (3 m) wide. That's the width of a trampoline!

The **capped heron** has long, thin feathers, called **plumes**, on its head, a blue and pink beak and a yellow neck. It is found near rivers and swamps in Central and South America.

The **Amazon kingfisher** has a shaggy head and blue-green wings. Males have a reddish-brown patch on their chest. They perch on branches and dive headfirst into the water to catch fish.

Layers of a Tropical Rainforest

Rainforests are divided into four main layers. Different plants and animals make up each layer.

The emergent layer is the highest layer, formed by the tops of the tallest trees. This layer gets the most sunlight and is full of fruits and flowers.

The canopy is the thick, leafy layer that grows high over the forest floor. The canopy is noisy because many forest animals live there.

The understory is the darker area under the canopy. It is full of small trees and shrubs, and tangled vines. Very little sunlight reaches the understory.

The forest floor is the bottom layer of a rainforest. It is damp, shady, quiet and covered in fallen leaves. Millions of insects live here.

RAINFOREST LAYERS

Emergent Layer

Canopy Layer

Understory Layer

Forest Floor

Life At the Top

The **emergent layer** is at the tops of the tallest trees in the rainforest. This layer gets the most sunlight, heat, wind and rain.

The emergent layer has towering trees that have straight trunks and wide, spreading branches. Kapok, rubber and Brazil nut trees are some of the tall trees found in the Amazon rainforest. Brazil nut trees can live to be 1000 years old!

Animals and insects move up and down between the different layers of forest. Some animals that might spend time in the emergent layer are harpy eagles, monkeys, macaws, toucans and morpho butterflies.

Towering Trees and Plenty of Plants

Have you ever noticed how fast plants grow in the summer? Plants grow well in warm, wet places like rainforests. The trees get very tall.

The upper tree branches spread out, blocking out sunlight to the forest floor. Down below, wide roots support the tall trees. The roots spread out sideways, anchoring the tree to the ground.

Climbing plants and vines twist up the tree trunks, reaching for sunlight. Lianas are the longest plants in the rainforest. These vines can grow hundreds of feet (meters) long!

Kapok Tree

Kapok trees, also called Ceiba trees, are some of the tallest trees in the Amazon rainforest. These trees can grow more than 200 feet (60 m) tall. That is the height of 3 red maple trees stacked on top of each other!

Kapok flowers are edible and taste like marshmallows! The stamens—the pointy stalks in the middle of the flower—are used to make food coloring for soups or curries.

Every part of the kapok trees is useful. The tree trunks are used to make canoes. The fluffy seed coverings are used in pillows, and seed oil is used to make soap. The seeds, bark and leaves are used in medicines, and the kapok roots can be roasted and eaten.

Harpy Eagle

Harpy eagles are large birds of prey that live in the treetops of the emergent layer. They have excellent eyesight and perch in the tall trees to watch for their prey.

Harpy eagles use their sharp talons, or claws, to grab prey. They eat monkeys, lizards and other animals. Sometimes they will swoop down into the canopy layer to hunt for sloths.

Eagle pairs build large nests. The nests are so big that 2 human adults could fit inside! These birds are found in Central and South America and can live to be 35 years old.

Toucans

Toucans are found high in treetops, in the rainforests of Central and South America. These birds can grow to be as big as a cat. A group of toucans is called a durante.

Toucans eat fruit, berries and nuts. They have huge, sharp beaks with jagged, knife-like edges. Their beaks are perfect for cutting up fruit or cracking nuts.

Toucans use their claws to grip branches. They have 4 toes on each foot, 2 pointing forward and 2 pointing backward.

Beautiful Butterflies

Thousands of kinds of butterflies live in the Amazon rainforest, from see-through glasswings to showy blue morphos. Butterflies fly through all the layers of the rainforest, from the treetops to the forest floor.

Blue morphos butterflies have shiny blue wings with tiny scales that reflect the light. The wings are dull brown underneath with black eyespots for distracting predators.

When the morpho flies, the bright blue and brown colors flash, and the butterfly seems to appear and disappear.

Average-sized trees with spreading branches form the canopy layer. This thick layer makes a living roof that does not let much sunlight through to the forest floor.

Green-headed Tanager

Squirrel Monkey

The canopy is the liveliest layer, where most animals live. It is full of noisy monkeys, slow-moving sloths, colorful birds, deadly snakes and many more unique animals and plants.

The Canopy

Until recently, life in the canopy was a mystery to scientists. Biologists, people who study animal and plant life, have built walkways high up between the trees, so they can study life in the canopy. Thousands of new species have been discovered.

Green Iguana

Sloths

Sloths are the slowest animals on Earth. They are found only in the rainforests of Central and South America.

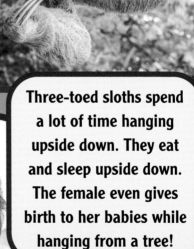

Three-toed sloths spend a lot of time hanging upside down. They eat and sleep upside down. The female even gives birth to her babies while hanging from a tree!

Sloths save energy by sleeping. They can sleep for 18 hours per day!

Sloths have long, curved claws that they hook around the branches to hang on and move from limb to limb. They rarely touch the ground. On land they use their claws to drag their bodies along. Surprisingly, sloths are good swimmers.

Many kinds of monkeys, apes and lemurs live in the rainforests. These animals are called primates. Humans are also primates!

Squirrel Monkey

Ring-tailed Lemurs

Primates

Some primates have opposable thumbs, so they can grasp things with their hands. Other animals, like dogs and cats, cannot use their paws to hold onto things.

Red Howler Monkey

Primates have large brains, long limbs, excellent eyesight and a good sense of smell.

Monkeys of the Amazon

About 130 different kinds of monkeys live in the Amazon rainforests, like howler monkeys, squirrel monkeys and capuchin monkeys.

Clever capuchin monkeys can use simple tools. They use stones to crack open nuts. They also use sponges made from mashed-up leaves to soak up food.

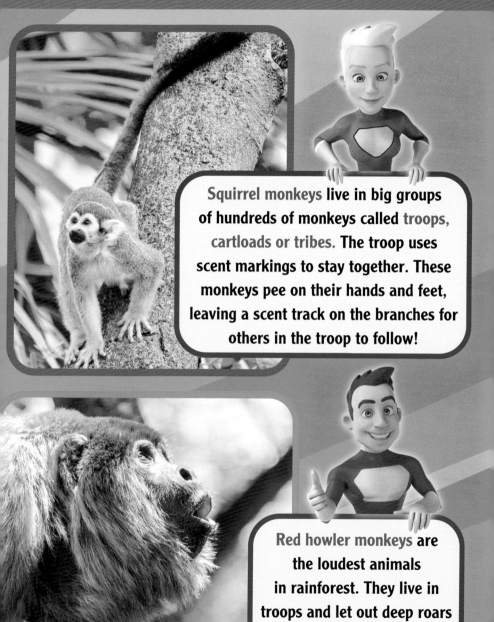

Squirrel monkeys live in big groups of hundreds of monkeys called troops, cartloads or tribes. The troop uses scent markings to stay together. These monkeys pee on their hands and feet, leaving a scent track on the branches for others in the troop to follow!

Red howler monkeys are the loudest animals in rainforest. They live in troops and let out deep roars to protect their territory.

There are about 160 monkey species living in the rainforests of Africa, including baboons, colobus monkeys and mandrills. Mandrills live deep in the rainforest. Males have bright blue and red markings on their faces. Mandrills are an endangered species. There are very few left in the world.

African Primates

To tell the difference between a monkey and an ape, look for a tail. Most monkeys have tails, but apes do not.

Gorillas live in the African rainforests. They are the largest primates, and they live in groups called troops, led by a large adult male. Gorillas sometimes climb trees, but they spend a lot of time on the ground playing, eating or resting.

Chimpanzees are found only in Africa. Chimpanzees are closely related to humans. Chimpanzees and gorillas in captivity can learn human languages, like American Sign Language. One female knew over 240 signs!

Lemurs

Ring-tailed Lemurs

Lemurs are possibly the cutest of the primates. These fuzzy, long-tailed creatures are found only on Madagascar, an island off the east coast of Africa. Lemurs are excellent at jumping through the treetops.

Ring-tailed Lemur

Mouse Lemur

Lemurs come in all shapes and sizes. Mouse lemurs are the tiniest lemurs and, like their name suggests, they are about the size of a mouse. Giant lemurs lived 1000 years ago and were the same size as gorillas!

Black-and-white ruffed lemur

Sadly, lemurs are some of the most endangered mammals in the world. Many species are close to extinction because the forests where they live are being cut down.

Diademed sifaka

Night Animals

Some of the animals in the Amazon rainforest are nocturnal. This means they spend most of the day sleeping and wake up at night to feed.

The Kinkajou, or honey bear, lives in the trees. It can climb down the trunk headfirst or run backwards along the branches. It slurps honey from beehives, using its long tongue.

Pygmy owls are tiny owls with round ears. They live in many rainforest habitats, from older forests to forest edges. They hunt at night for insects and spiders.

Like many nocturnal animals, owl monkeys have huge eyes to help them see in the dark. Owl monkeys do not see in color. They can only see in shades of gray. This helps them find their prey at night.

Parrots and Macaws

Parrots are colorful birds that come in all sizes. Macaws are a kind of parrot. The hyacinth macaw lives in Central and South America. It is the largest parrot in the world and can grow to be 3 feet (1 m) tall. That's as tall as a large dog!

Parrots have strong beaks that they use to crack open the nuts, seeds and fruit they eat. Their long tails are half the length of their bodies!

A group of parrots is called a pandemonium, and a group of macaws is called an endangerment. Parrots and macaws can be seen eating clay along riverbanks in the Amazon! Clay is a source of sodium, a nutrient that animals need to grow and stay healthy.

Emerald Tree Boa

The emerald tree boa is a strong and silent snake that eats birds and small animals. It coils around a branch and lies in wait, leaving its mouth free to strike at a passing bird or rodent.

This snake lives in the canopy. Its green color helps it hide among the leaves.

Boa constrictors wrap themselves around their prey, squeeze tightly and then swallow their prey whole.

Emerald tree boas do not lay eggs like other snakes. Instead, they give birth to live babies. Young snakes are born with red skin that turns green as they get older.

Rubber Tree

Did you know that rubber comes from a tree? Rubber is used to make many things, including tires, rubber gloves, clothing, rubber bands and balloons. It was first discovered thousands of years ago by the Indigenous Peoples of Central and South America.

Rubber is made from a white liquid called latex. The latex is tapped from the stem of the rubber tree, just like maple syrup is tapped from a maple tree. When exposed to air, the latex thickens into solid rubber!

Today, most natural rubber comes from plantations in South Asia. People also use artificial rubber that is made in factories.

Bromeliads

Bromeliads are a group of plants that grow high in the canopy. These plants have thick, waxy leaves that grow in a circle. A pineapple is in the bromeliad family.

The bromeliad leaves catch raindrops. The rain is funnelled to center of the plant, where tiny ponds form. Monkeys and birds drink from these pools. Insects or tadpoles may live in them.

Most plants grow on the ground and get their nutrients from the soil. Bromeliads are air plants, called epiphytes. They usually grow on tree trunks or branches and get their food and water from the air.

Orchids

Orchids are beautiful flowers that come in many colors and sizes. They can be white, pink, orange, purple or yellow. Their bright colors help the orchid stand out, so pollinating insects can find them.

There are more than 20,000 kinds of orchids in the world. Among flowering plants, only sunflowers have more varieties.

Half of all orchids are epiphytes. Like bromeliads, they live high in the rainforest canopy. They stretch their white roots over the branches to take up as much water as possible when it rains. The water is stored in their thick leaves.

Rainforest conditions are perfect for orchids. The flowers can bloom for months.

The Understory

Imagine you are standing on the ground in a tropical rainforest, looking around. You see small trees, shrubs and vines, in many shades of green with leaves of every shape and size. You are looking at the forest understory.

The understory gets little sunlight. It is shady because the thick canopy blocks out most of the sunlight.

The rainforest is full of sounds. There are buzzing insects, rythmic toads and singing birds. The forest is still noisy after the sun goes down. Many creatures are active at night.

Cocoa Tree

Did you know that chocolate grows on trees? Chocolate is made from cocoa beans, the seeds of cocoa trees.

Cocoa trees are small trees that grow in the shaded understory. They grow in the rainforests of Mexico and South America. Today, cocoa trees are also grown on plantations in other tropical countries.

Cocoa seeds have a bitter taste. To make chocolate, the seeds must be fermented, dried, cleaned and roasted. The hard shell is removed, and the seeds are ground into cocoa. The cocoa is then heated into a liquid with other ingredients, like sugar and milk, to make chocolate.

Tangled Vines and Strangling Roots

The rainforest understory is filled with plants that have adapted to the shade and find unique ways to get water and sunlight.

Lianas are long, woody vines that loop around other plants and grow up toward the light. Lianas make natural bridges between the trees that animals can run on.

The **strangler fig** is a **parasitic** plant that grows on a **host** tree. The fig starts growing near the top of a tree, after a monkey or bird drops a sticky seed onto a tree branch. It then sends roots down to the ground, often surrounding the host tree.

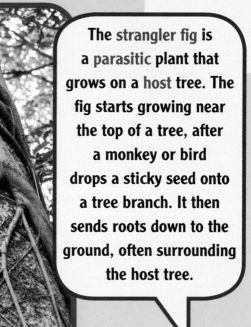

The host tree may die if it cannot get enough sunlight and water, leaving only the roots of the strangler fig.

Bats

Bats are the most plentiful mammals in the rainforest. Half of all mammal species in the rainforests are bats. Most bats eat insects, but some eat fruit or blood.

Brazilian
long-nosed bat

Bats that eat insects usually hunt at night using echolocation. They make squeaky sounds, and the sound bounces off nearby objects and echos back when it hits an object like an insect.

Greater Spear-nosed Bat

Common Vampire Bat

Vampire bats live in Central and South America. Some people fear them because they feed on the blood of animals. These bats mostly feed on cow blood. They rarely bite people. Oddly, vampire bats land far away from their prey and approach on foot.

Hoatzin

The hoatzin, pronounced *HWAT-sin*, is sometimes called stink bird. Hoatzins live near rivers and lakes in the Amazon rainforest.

Hoatzins eat leaves. It takes them a few days to digest or break down their food. After a while, the leaves sitting in their digestive system start to stink. And so do the hoatzins when they let out smelly burps!

These large, loud birds live in groups called dongles and are easy to find along wetlands. They spend a lot of time sitting in trees, but they are not strong fliers.

Green Iguana

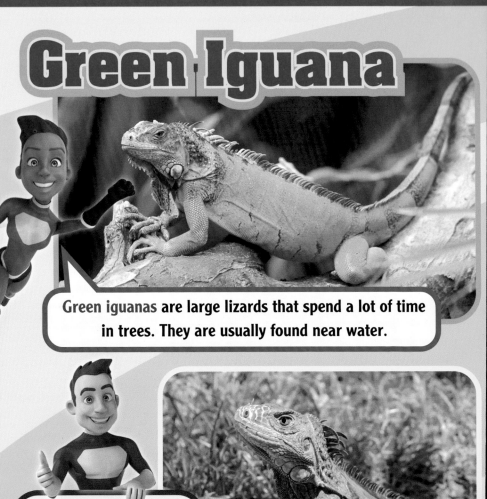

Green iguanas are large lizards that spend a lot of time in trees. They are usually found near water.

Lizards are cold-blooded creatures, using their surroundings to control their body temperature. They bask in the sun to warm up and cool off in the shade.

Green Iguanas can change color, from green to blue-gray, brown or turquoise. Breeding males can even be orange. When they are cold, their color darkens to help the iguana absorb heat. As the lizard warms up, its color lightens.

The green iguana has a third eye on top of its head! This small eye is different than the lizard's other eyes. It senses movement and light to help the lizard see predators, like hawks or owls, swooping in from above.

Frog and Toads

Frogs and toads can look similar. Both live in the rainforest, usually near water. Frogs have triangular heads and long legs. Toads have bumpy skin, round heads and short legs.

Tree frogs have long legs and sticky toe pads to help them climb wet, slippery leaves. The red-eyed tree frog hunts at night, catching insects with its long, sticky tongue. Its big, red eyes scare predators.

Poison dart frogs are tiny, brightly colored frogs with poisonous skin. Their bright colors warn predators not to eat them. Indigenous Peoples use the deadly toxins from the dart frog's skin to make poison-tipped arrows for hunting.

The cane toad is a large toad that lives in the Amazon rainforest. The cane toad was introduced in other places, like Australia, to eat insects in sugarcane fields. It has become a pest there because it has no predators.

The Forest Floor

The forest floor is dark and filled with mosses and ferns. Fungi break down the decaying leaves. Jaguars hide in the shadows, and insect-eating animals search for food.

Surprisingly, the rainforests floor has only a thin layer of soil. The soil is not very fertile because the large plants and trees use up all the nutrients in the soil.

Pitcher plants grow in swampy areas. These carnivorous plants eat insects. Flies land on the plant's slippery edges and then fall into pools of juice. The juice digests the insects, turning them into nutrients for the plant!

Jaguar

Jaguars are large cats that live in the jungles of Central and South America. They often hide in trees, waiting to pounce on their prey.

These fierce cats hunt at night and prey on animals like tapir or deer. They have strong jaws and sharp teeth. They can kill their prey with one bite.

Tapir

Tapirs look like a pig with a long snout. They use their short trunk, or snout, to help them catch the scent of predators. They also use their snouts like elephants do, picking leaves off trees to eat.

Most tapirs are found in the rainforests of Central and South America.

Tapirs are good swimmers. They spend time in the water to cool off and to hide from jaguars. When a tapir dives underwater, it uses its snout like a snorkel to breath.

A baby tapir is camouflaged with spots and stripes to help it hide among grass and leaves.

Armies of Ants

There are 30 million different insects living in the rainforest and thousands of different kinds of ants!

Ants live in groups called colonies. Some colonies can have millions of ants. Ant colonies may be underground, on the ground in mounds, or in trees.

Army ants feed on small animals and insects. They march in long lines, eating everything in their path. To rest, they make a shelter out of their own bodies!

Leafcutter ants march in long lines up and down tree trunks. They use their sharp jaws to cut pieces of leaves and carry them back to the nest.

Giants of the Forest Floor

The Goliath birdeater of South America is the largest tarantula in the world. It is almost as big as a dinner plate! It mainly eats insects, worms and frogs, but has been known to eat lizards, birds and small rodents.

The Goliath birdeater lives in a burrow. It has 8 eyes, but it doesn't see well. Instead, this spider spins fine silk around its burrow, and when an animal is nearby it can feel the vibrations in the silk threads. The spider then springs out and grabs its prey.

Huge centipedes live in rainforests around the world. The Amazon giant centipede is the world's largest centipede. It feeds on insects or small animals, like lizards and mice!

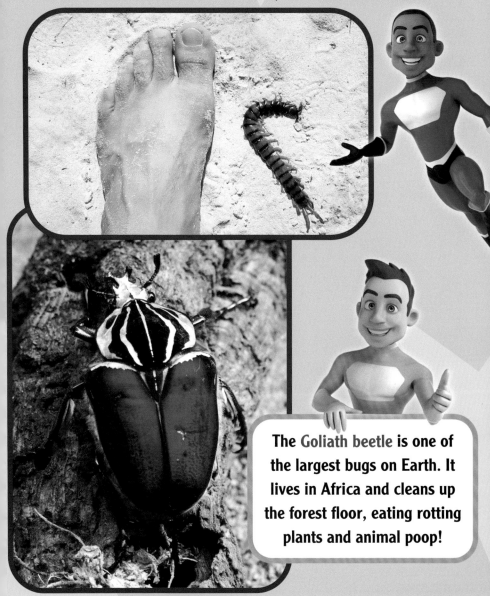

The Goliath beetle is one of the largest bugs on Earth. It lives in Africa and cleans up the forest floor, eating rotting plants and animal poop!

Indigenous Peoples

People are also part of the ecosystem. Indigenous Peoples have lived in the rainforests for thousands of years. They play an important role in protecting the land.

Tribes like the Yanomami, Kayapo and Tupi-Guarani Peoples have lived in the Amazon for more than 32,000 years!

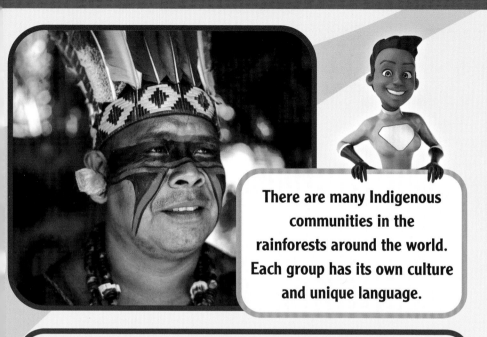

There are many Indigenous communities in the rainforests around the world. Each group has its own culture and unique language.

Traditionally, Indigenous Peoples relied on the forest for food, medicine and shelter. Today many still depend on the forests but have changed their lives to include modern ways.

Changing Lifestyles

Indigenous Peoples often moved from place to place, following a food source. Groups sometimes settled for a short time near water to fish and hunt the animals living there.

Other tribes, like the Tupi-Guarani people of Brazil, lived in large villages along the coast. The Tupi were one of the first tribes European explorers met when they arrived in South America about 500 years ago.

Some tribes in the Amazon still live in isolation deep within the rainforests.

Vanishing Rainforests

Rainforests are full of amazing creatures and plants. They are important to the health of our planet. They provide food, water, shelter and medicine for people and animals. Tropical rainforests are sometimes called the lungs of the world because they produce much of the world's oxygen!

But rainforests are vanishing. The trees are being cut down for farming, logging, mining and fuel. Every day, 25,000 square miles (65,000 square km) of rainforests are cut down. That's the size 74,000 soccer fields or the state of West Virginia!

The soil in the rainforest is poor, with few nutrients. Once the trees are gone, the land is not good for farming. It can take more than 100 years for the trees to grow back.

Protecting the Rainforests

People are working to protect the rainforests. National parks and forest preserves protect these beautiful areas and the plants and animals that live there.

Educational and ecotourism programs teach people about the rainforests and Indigenous cultures.

The Publisher: Super Explorers is an imprint of Blue Bike Books

Library and Archives Canada Cataloguing in Publication

Title: Exploring tropical rainforests / Krista Kagume.

Names: Kagume, Krista, author.

Identifiers: Canadiana (print) 20220206376 | Canadiana (ebook) 20220206384 | ISBN 9781989209189 (softcover) | ISBN 9781989209196 (PDF)

Subjects: LCSH: Rain forests—Juvenile literature. | LCSH: Rain forest ecology—Juvenile literature.

Classification: LCC QH86 .K34 2022 | DDC j577.34—dc23

Front cover credit: Getty Image, Ondrej Prosicky

Back cover credits: Tamara Hartson, Getty Images Gary Gray, Getty Images reptiles4all.

Photo Credits: From Getty Images: 12MN 90, aaprophoto 40a, ABDESIGN 76b, Abinormal 78-79, Aleksandr_Vorobev 37b, alex grichenko 49a, Allan Watson 74b, AmandaTomkins 51b, ANDREYGUDKOV 49b, Anibal Pabon 29c, ANPerryman 63a, Anton Sorokin 56b, Apiwan Borrikonratchata 11a, Atelopus 64a, atosan 33a, Aulia Maghfiroh 75b, bahadir-yeniceri 38b, bAllllAd 16b, BrianAbrahamson 57b, bridge99 65b, Charlie Fayers 55a, Christian Vinces 15a, Connah 65a, Connah 73a, Connie Pinson 69b, daboost 17a, Damian Lugowski 79b, Damocean 17b, Dan Olsen 86, DC_Colombia 47b, dennisvdw 51a, Dmytro Yarmolin 6, Dreamframer 87a, EcoVentures-Travel 54, ekolara 32a, Enrico Pescantini 42a, estivillml 2-3, Fatima Freitas 43b, Fernando Alonso Stock Films 14, filipefrazao 88, filipefrazao 89ab, filipefrazao 91a, Gaardman 72, Gab13 85b, Gabriel Mendes 71ab, Gary Gray 39a, Gleb_Ivanov 68, GlobalP 45a, Grigorii_Pisotckii 21a, halbrindley 44b, hsvrs 74a, ieang 62a, jacoblund 9, JarnoVerdonk 12b, jez_bennett 50b, John Carnemolla 77b, Jonathan Ross 11b, Jrleyland 76a, Ken Griffiths 69a, kikkerdirk 77a, Kirsten Dunlap 62b, kompasstudio 8-9, kwiktor 81b, Laralrimeeva 10b, Ledernase 58, Leo Sagayaraj 42b, LESSY SEBASTIAN 48, Luis Arce 95b, M&M 34, Manakin 23b, Mark Kostich 43a, Mark Kostich 5a, Mark Kostich 82ab, MarkMalkinsonPhotography 83b, Mathias Möller 53b, mayskyphoto 12a, mdurajczyk 60b, michaklootwijk 83a, Michel VIARD 22, Michel VIARD 23a, migadi 40b, MikeLane45 46b, miroslav_1 29b, miroslav_1 4-5, miroslav_1 94-95, mumifikator 63b, Naeblys 7, NirutiStock 92-93, nodramallama 20b, NTCo 13b, ok-sana 32bcd, OlgaKlyushina 84, Ondrej Prosicky 36ab, Ondrej Prosicky 5b, Paralaxis 28, PaulMaguire 50a, Pere_Rubi 41a, peterspiro 39b, Petmal 10a, pgbrace 35a, quickshooting 31a, Ramdan_Nain 30, rchphoto 91b, reptiles4all 13a, reptiles4all 57a, RichLindie 25a, Rudzhan Nagiev 27, sabelskaya 8, Salinger 61a, SHAWSHANK61 87b, silverjohn 75a, slowmotiongli 20a, Smithore 31b, STILLFX 40-41, STILLFX 6-7, STILLFX 64-65, Tanarch 67ab, tane-mahuta 42c, Tarcisio Schnaider 29a, Tarcisio Schnaider 93b, TatianaMironenko 21b, tewin 59b, timspix58 56a, Tom Brakefield 52, Tristan Barrington Photography 53a, Tristan Barrington Photography 73b, TT 84, undefined undefined 60a, underverse 59a, VitalyEdush 47a, Waldemar Seehagen 38a, webguzs 44a, webguzs 45b, webguzs 46a, williamhc 61b, xeni4ka 15b. From Wikimedia Commons: Bernard DUPONT 25b, J.M.Garg 32, H. Zell 33b, Michael Hogan 51c, Brian Ralphs 55b, KATHERINE WAGNER-REISS 66, Pavel Kirillov 85a. From Flickr: The Next Gen Scientist 35b. From Tamara Hartson: 4, 18ab, 19ab, 24ab, 37a, 41b, 70, 80ab, 81a.

Superhero Illustrations: julos/Thinkstock.

Produced with the assistance of the Government of Alberta.

We acknowledge the financial support of the Government of Canada.

Nous reconnaissons l'appui financier du gouvernement du Canada.

Funded by the Government of Canada
Financé par le gouvernement du Canada |

Printed in China
PC: 38-1